THE FIELD GUIDE

*Finding Your Way Through
a Difficult Diagnosis*

by Barbara Jandu, M.A.

KDP Publishing

ISBN: 9798856457925

Cover art by: Renée Switkes

Library of Congress Control Number: 2018675309
Printed in the United States of America

This work is dedicated:

to my kind and patient husband who saw me through the darkest of times;

to my two beloved sons who were both inspirational and instrumental in helping me survive;

to my closest friends and tribe, who checked in on me, encouraged me, and held faith with me.

It is my hope that what I have learned will be helpful to so many who feel unseen in their difficult circumstances. You are more than your struggle; you are a wonderful creation; you can do this.

CONTENTS

INTRODUCTION

In November 2022, I was given a life-threatening diagnosis that turned my world upside-down. I had just arrived home from having some medical tests done. Before I even stepped through the door, our landline was ringing! Feeling something was amiss, I answered it right away. On the other end of the phone was my primary care physician. My heart sank as my mind tried to absorb the gravity of the situation as she described it. She told me to go immediately to the nearest emergency room. I barely had time to grab a quick bite to eat, throw a few items into my straw bag, and rush out the door with my husband.

Once we arrived at the hospital, I called two of my friends. One stayed with me on the phone, praying for a miracle; the other came to the hospital to sit with me while my husband went to pick up our youngest son from his band performance. I can still remember the look on my husband's face as we discussed how to tell our two teenaged sons that the things we thought of as normal... so many things we had taken for granted... were all about to change, and we didn't know for how long.

It took three excruciating hours of waiting in the emergency room to finally be seen by a specialist and admitted. I was not the only person needing urgent medical care that night. This was at a time when both RSV (respiratory syncytial virus) and COVID-19 cases were on the rise; there were over 70 people waiting with me. I can still vividly remember some patients being brought in by ambulance with what looked like very painful injuries from accidents. Others were coughing uncontrollably. What broke my heart the most were the children who were exhausted from vomiting as they continued to wait for much-needed medical attention.

As I finally lay in my hospital bed late that night, listening to monitors beeping, I was so thankful that I had been given the very last room available. My nurse administered an I.V. with all sorts of medications, then told me to get some rest. What people don't tell you is that this is nearly impossible. The lights remained bright in the hallway all night long. Hospital staff chatted loudly outside my door. A nurse came in every couple of hours to check my vital signs or give me more medicine.

Early the next morning, I was carted away from my room for the first of many times for testing.

When my sons were finally able to visit, my oldest brought his guitar and sang to me; my youngest brought a stuffed animal to keep me company; and my husband brought my eye mask so I could finally get some sleep!

I only shed tears once during that hospital stay. It was when I heard that I would need to go on indefinite medical leave from my job. For the record, I am usually the first person to remind my friends and family that each of us is more than what we do. But, this... somehow seemed different in that moment. Up until that point, I was working as a psychotherapist and felt tremendous meaning and purpose in helping others. I loved my clients and knowing I would have to leave them, albeit in good hands, was heartbreaking.

Mine had been a long journey toward reaching this point in my career. For years, I had been fascinated by human behavior and the potential that exists within each person to overcome seemingly insurmountable obstacles in order to achieve wholeness and stability. But life took me in a different direction for quite some time. After many years of working in corporate America, I decided to return to college. This was just after my first son started preschool. I continued part-time, balancing marriage, kiddos, home, and school until I was finally able to begin my dream job in earnest. And here I was, in a hospital bed, being told this part of my life - indeed most parts of my life - would be on hold indefinitely.

I was in that hospital bed for a total of four days. Those days were filled with a whirlwind of tests, scans, and a lot of waiting for answers. Despite all of this, I kept thinking to myself how different medical trauma is from other types of trauma. I also found myself experiencing an unexplainable, transcendent sense of peace. I determined in those moments that I would not give up.

The first several weeks back at home were a blur. As I awaited the results of more testing, my condition steadily declined. I remember lying on the sofa, wondering what might happen; I prayed that I would live long enough to see my boys grow up, get married, and have children of their own. With that in mind, I knew I needed to do whatever I could to prepare myself for the battle to come. So I adopted the mindset of a warrior – because I began to realize this battle would not only be physical, but mental, emotional, and spiritual as well.

When I finally began treatments in December, I came to understand that whatever my future held, it was certain to bring with it many challenges. That is when I found myself wishing for instructions or some sort of handbook on how to get through all I had to face. The concepts in this little book are neither new nor mine alone. It is an amalgamation of others' wisdom and even professional advice I myself had passed along to clients; insights that, as a result of my condition, I had ample opportunity to put into practice. It is also a result of the many words of inspiration I received over the next several months after my diagnosis.

My main purpose here is to bring comfort and provide coping strategies for those who find themselves in similar circumstances; those who are facing life-altering diagnoses, chronic invisible illnesses, or a whole host of other situations that leave someone feeling like the wind has been knocked out of them. Whether short-term or long-term, situations such as these can be devastating. They can also be a catalyst for growth in some remarkable ways.

If you've picked up this book or were given it as a gift, please know that it is my sincere wish for you to be encouraged. There are a number of spiritual practices I have found helpful in my journey, but if that's not you, you may still find it a worthwhile read. Glean what you can, take whatever is useful, and either leave the rest or perhaps consider it with an open mind. When dealing with a difficult diagnosis or some other medical mayhem, the road to recovery can be paved with hope, and even joy. This book is here to offer you some ideas that you may find helpful during your own challenging circumstances.

WAKING UP WORTHY

"By simply changing the way you wake up in the morning, you can transform any area of your life, faster than you ever thought possible."

HAL ELROD

I believe that each and every one of us is worthy of being treated with respect and dignity automatically because we're all created in God's image. So why is it, especially in difficult times, that we are so hard on ourselves?

Speaking from experience, I can attest to the fact that if you allow yourself to become convinced – even for a moment – that you don't deserve to be here, this battle you are facing will become even more daunting than is necessary. I found that on my most difficult days, it was that much more important for me to find just a little sliver of light or joy.

For you, it might mean that some days you simply take delight in being able to brush your teeth. Other days, it could be celebrating that you saw a beautiful sunset or woke up to hear birds chirping. And sometimes, a positive self-greeting could be just the oomph you need to get out of bed.

When I was in grad school, my positive psychology professor, Dr. Shauna Shapiro, once shared how her therapist advised that she do something rather awkward each morning. She instructed Dr. Shapiro that, upon waking, she should greet herself with the words, "Good morning, Shauna. I love you." My professor went on to describe how uncomfortable this was for her at first, but with practice it got easier over time. She eventually embraced the concept so fully that she went on to write a book entitled, *Good Morning, I Love You*. Similarly, former First Lady Michelle Obama writes in her book *All the Light We Carry* about her friend Ron. Ron wakes up every morning and greets himself in the mirror with an enthusiastic "Heeey, Buddy!".

Now I don't know about you, but I am not a morning person, even on my best days. Once I get going, I can usually find a word of encouragement or friendly greeting for other people. But greeting myself this way? That felt so weird! Occasionally, I'd try the "I love you" approach but found myself settling on "I am loved", which felt more authentic for me personally. It took a little experimentation, but eventually I decided upon the following positive affirmations for myself each morning:

I am okay.
I am good enough.
I am safe.
I am loved.
I am not alone.
God is *for* me.
I have choices.
It's okay to just be.
I can do this.
I am confident, protected, and guarded.
I can remember the lessons learned.
I can believe for big miracles.

This is a practice I had introduced to some of my clients long before I got my diagnosis. It took me quite some time before I realized that it was okay, necessary even, to take my own advice. Giving myself permission to treat myself as someone who is deserving of kindness - that's what I mean by learning how to wake up worthy.

FINDING
YOUR TRIBE

*"Many people want to ride with you in the limo, but
you want someone who will take the bus with you
when the limo breaks down."*

OPRAH WINFREY

You may have heard the old adage, "It takes
a village". Villages all across the world are filled
with tribe members. In Western society, this tribe
mentality is often missing. When finding your
tribe, you may notice that some are actual family
members but others are not. Among your circle of
friends, you may even find some who you consider
to be chosen family. Do not underestimate the value
of these trusting relationships. These are the safe
people whose support will be paramount in getting
you through this difficult season.

In our most trying times, it's important to distinguish between safe people and those who are not as healthy for us. In his book *Safe People*, Dr. Henry Cloud writes, "People with a style of denial and blaming are definitely on the list of unsafe people to avoid." His co-author, Dr. John Townsend, writes in *The Entitlement Cure*, "Some of the nicest people in the world are also total flakes. They can be caring, well-intentioned, and thoughtful. Yet at the same time, they can be undependable and unreliable."

Safe people, as Cloud and Townsend describe, are empathetic, admit their weaknesses, are open to your feedback, and take responsibility for their own actions. They are not judgmental and when they do need to confront you with the truth as they see it, they do so with love and grace. They exhibit consistency and authenticity over time, and don't try to rush a relationship. Safe people respect boundaries and maintain confidentiality. In short, these are people with whom it's safe to be vulnerable.

According to author, research professor, and podcast host Dr. Brené Brown, vulnerability is sharing with people who've "earned the right to hear our stories and experiences". Furthermore she states that we need to "walk through vulnerability to get to courage". In her 2019 Netflix special, *The*

Call to Courage, she discusses how to do just that.

When assembling your list of safe people, choose those who have done enough of their own psychological work to stay present with you. You'll need members of your tribe to validate your feelings without overreacting or offering unsolicited advice, and definitely without making it all about them. People who can convey hope, respect, and encouragement while holding space and gently offering different perspectives are worth their weight in gold! These are your people – this is your tribe.

ALLOWING FOR ALTRUISM

*"Giving feels fantastic and for there to be a Giver,
there must be a Receiver, so allowing yourself to
receive is an act of love."*

REBECCA O'DWYER

Psychology professor Dr. Stephanie D. Preston defines altruism as a motivational state in which the goal is to increase another person's welfare without conscious regard to one's own personal interests. Even more specifically, altruistic responding refers to help that is motivated by seeing someone in need or distress.

The practice of altruistic responding comes with many benefits for the giver. These include positive mood, happiness, life satisfaction, better physical health, and overall well-being. Evidence of these benefits have been noted by several researchers over the years, leading to the conclusion that it truly is more of a blessing to be able to give than to receive.

Even knowing that it feels good for others to give, when we're hit with life's challenges, many of us still often struggle to ask for the help we need. Some of us are concerned about being a burden to others. Some of us might fear appearing too needy. But what if we looked at it from a completely different perspective? In her research, UCLA psychology professor Dr. Naomi Eisenberger found that when a person helps someone else, the reward center of the helper's brain lights up in a similar way as when experiencing pleasures like sex or chocolate. Helping people boosts the helper's immunity too; it even reduces their stress hormones.

When you do reach out to ask for help, there are a few things to keep in mind. First of all, don't apologize. This will only serve to reduce the helper's positive feelings. Secondly, ask directly for what you need. Being specific about your requests will alleviate the need for your friends and family members to try and read your mind. And finally, be authentic. Allowing yourself to be vulnerable enough with the people in your tribe to ask them for specific help is a gift to them as well as to yourself. Beyond that, you may find that people respond favorably to your authenticity – it gives them permission to be themselves with you also.

Of course, be aware of which person you ask for which favor. You certainly wouldn't want to ask for a meal from your friend who doesn't cook or request help with transportation from your colleague who gets nervous whenever there's another person in the car. Take into consideration each person's talents, interests, and financial situation. If possible, asking in-person seems to lead to more favorable responses than emails, but do what feels best for your situation.

After you have received what you need, it's lovely to offer sincere gratitude. You can even support local artists by purchasing their thank you cards. Whether a handwritten note or an email of gratitude, it's nice to be specific about how the person helped you. These notes will show just how much you value and care about your tribe.

Finally, when you are feeling better or even just having a good day, you might decide to pay it forward. You may choose to volunteer as a mentor. Or perhaps you'll put together a *Meal Train* or *SignUpGenius* to help someone else in need. Even giving your understanding presence to a friend going through something similar to what you just overcame can be beneficial for both of you.

CARING FOR THE CAREGIVERS

"When you are a caregiver, you know that every day you will touch a life and a life will touch yours."

ANONYMOUS

You may not be in a position to provide physical care for those helping you during this time, but there are things you can do to encourage your caregiver(s) to maintain their own positive self-care routine, which in turn will also help you.

Research psychologist Dr. Kristen Neff writes on her website how important it is for caregivers to meet their own needs so that they have the energy for those relying on them. She includes suggestions like yoga or time with friends that can be done away from the person they're helping as well as "on the job" ideas such as self-massage or an open-hearted conversation about how overwhelmed both you and your caregiver(s) can feel sometimes. In order to help them help you, here are a few suggestions on how to interact with your caregivers.

Communicate Calmly

"Gracious words are a honeycomb, sweet to
the soul and healing to the bones."
~Jewish Proverb

I am the first to admit that communicating effectively and considerately is extra difficult when I am in pain or hungry or feeling impatient. The acronym that's helped our family the most is WIN. It stands for:

"When _____,
I feel _____.
I need _____."

Some people also add another N for Negotiate, to help you agree on how, when, and to what degree that need can be met. The first step is to identify our own ever-elusive emotions. Emotions serve a number of purposes. Although they are transient and ever-changing, feelings can help us identify needs and values, connect with other humans, and even make logical decisions. Logic? Oh yes! Logic and emotion are not on opposite teams. In fact, if someone suffers an injury to their limbic system (the emotional part of the brain) it can actually impact that person's ability to even decide what to eat for breakfast!

Despite societal messaging, men and women have access to all of the same emotions. There is some disagreement among psychological professionals as to which are in the list of core emotions, but generally speaking, they include: glad sad, mad afraid, disgusted, and surprised. They get more nuanced from there, but this is a good starting lineup.

We humans tend to wrestle with our emotions in a variety of ways. Sometimes, we bury our feelings only to have them come out at inconvenient times or in unhealthy ways. Other times, we might completely disconnect from what we're feeling. And sometimes, we can only identify one primary emotion that feels safe enough to express (usually anger). Whatever your particular struggle, there are some concrete ways to make peace with these emotions that can, at times, seem overwhelming; by choosing to use them for their intended purposes.

Step 1 - Become Aware

It can be hard to identify emotions, especially when you get stuck in your head, so to speak. At times like those, it helps to check in with your body. Artist and former therapist Lindsay Braman has developed a handy Emotion-Sensation Wheel that I find useful. Doing a quick body scan can elicit some information also. For example, if you're looking down, shoulders slumped, and have a lump in your throat, there may be some sadness. If your shoulders are tense, stomach is churning, and hands are sweating, that could indicate you're feeling fearful or anxious in that moment. Just find the general feeling and then get more specific until you land on one that fits.

Step 2: Acknowledge Them

From there, you can "name it to tame it'". Name what you are feeling in the moment. You can try saying to yourself, "I'm feeling _____ right now". You might even notice that part of you feels one way and another part feels differently. That's okay. Just name what you notice. For those of us who grew up without having our feelings acknowledged, this can be hard but very healing.

Step 3: Allow Them to Be

This step can be like a soothing balm for your soul. To simply allow your feelings to be, to exist, without judgment or trying to change them is so fruitful and freeing! Acknowledge the courage it takes to just sit mindfully with whatever comes up without trying to fix it or change it. Just *be*.

Step 4: Identify the Underlying Needs

Nonviolent Communication trainers Jim and Jori Manske developed a helpful Needs Wheel that I keep handy for our whole family to use whenever one of us gets stumped. It helps to identify what's really essential; what's under the emotions.

Even without looking at a needs chart, you can try naming an opposite emotion of the difficult one you're experiencing. If I'm feeling sad, for example, I can ask myself, "What would bring me a little joy?". If I'm feeling tense or stressed, I can think of things that might bring me a sense of peace or calm. Try it! In many cases, you will be surprised at how you can do something right then to feel better. If your need isn't an "easy fix", this information will at the very least be useful in making a plan to communicate your needs at a time that feels right.

Step 5: Express Them

Even if you were able to meet your own needs after following the first four steps, telling a safe person how you felt can be wonderful! Trusted people in our lives can also help meet some of those needs. Expressing authentic emotions and needs, in a gentle way, can make this easier for our people. Researchers at the Gottman Institute call this type of communication the Softened Startup.

Appreciate Abundantly

"Gratitude is riches. Complaint is poverty."
~Doris Day

The other day, I was talking to my sons about the definitions of the words appreciate and depreciate. According to Oxford's English Dictionary, the word appreciate means to "recognize the full worth of" someone or something. In contrast, the word depreciate means "to decrease in value over a period of time". We usually think of items that depreciate over time, like a car or a toaster.

But if we're not careful, we can grow to take people for granted over time also, rather than seeing their true value. Perhaps as we express appreciation to our caregivers, family, and friends (without apologizing for our needs), it may also allow each of us to see ourselves as less of a burden. This subtle shift in perspective may even change the dynamic between you and your caregiver in a more positive and healthy direction.

Remember that viewing yourself as an equal in need of help makes the hearty, "Thank you for

_____" a lot easier than seeing yourself as a nuisance. In this way, you simultaneously recognize your caregiver's full worth as well as your own.

Encourage Enthusiastically

Encourage: "to inspire with courage, spirit, or hope"
~Merriam-Webster Dictionary

It was such a moment of insight when I was finally able to put myself in each of my family member's shoes; to really contemplate what my diagnosis meant to each of them. In doing so, I had to be very careful not to let this morph into me feeling guilty. I certainly did not get sick on purpose and shaming myself would only have lessened my ability to empathize with them. By giving myself space to contemplate how my situation was affecting our family, I was able to be more patient and compassionate toward myself and each of them also.

When you are able, you can try letting your caregiver know, through words and empathy, that it's okay to be imperfect. You're in this together and you're both learning. Mistakes are how we all learn. The people in our lives are not going to get it right every time. Be as patient with them as you are learning to be with yourself. Encourage your caregivers to give themselves permission to take a break and especially to develop a regular self-care routine. Give the same kindness that you would want to receive if you were in your caregiver's shoes.

It might seem odd to contemplate yourself as the one being an encouragement to your caregiver(s), but never underestimate the power of your perseverance and hopeful attitude.

TRUSTING
YOUR TEAM

"Nothing in life is to be feared, it is only to be understood. Now is the time to understand more, so that we may fear less."

MARIE CURIE

First of all, we need to acknowledge that not everyone has the same access to excellent medical care. Check with your insurance or health plan provider to find out which doctors and facilities you can access. Search up patient reviews and choose the very best medical team you can afford. Then trust them. Follow their guidance. If you have questions, don't hesitate to ask. Work with them to determine the best course of action. I have found that nurse practitioners are especially valuable resources, although they're often underutilized.

I have always been tremendously interested in human biology. Although I find other forms of science intriguing, I have a long-held philosophy that because I exist daily within this body of mine, I should know as much about how it functions as humanly possible. The limited understanding I have managed to accumulate over the years has proved to be a springboard for my curiosity. Especially through some of my darkest times, I found that a willingness to find out what I didn't know about my diagnosis led me to ask my medical team the right questions. If you either don't possess this natural curiosity or simply don't have the energy to seek out medical information, perhaps someone in your tribe might be willing to help you navigate.

With that, I would like to provide a word of caution. Not every remedy you hear from well-meaning friends or read on social media will be applicable to your situation. If you or your trusted tribe members do choose to consult the internet, I recommend looking for scholarly, peer-reviewed medical journal articles (available on Google Scholar) and articles published by well-established medical colleges such as Johns Hopkins, the Mayo Clinic, Stanford, or similar institutions.

Your medical team may want you to keep track of vital signs, symptoms, or medication side effects. Take this seriously. Depending on what ails you, keeping a food diary might also be helpful.

Reach out to your tribe if you need help. By participating in your own healthcare, you are a valuable source of information.

STANDING IN SELF-COMPASSION

*"Self-compassion is simply giving the same kindness
to ourselves that we would give to others."*

CHRISTOPHER GERMER

Different diagnoses come with different symptoms. Treatments and medications all have side effects. All of this takes patience and adjustment. Judging oneself while already struggling simply isn't beneficial.

Among her dozens of studies on the subject, Dr. Kristen Neff found that self-compassion is even more powerful than self-esteem because it allows us to get back up again without needing to achieve a sense of perfection. Instead, when we are able to give ourselves grace and speak to ourselves as we would a dear friend, this invites freedom, growth, and learning. We can't learn very well when we're in a state of shame.

If you grew up with critical parents, harsh teachers, or peers who bullied you, this may take some time. Understanding the role of your internalized critic and then meeting that voice with calm curiosity can be a good first step.

There are several exercises that I've found helpful on Dr. Neff's self-compassion website. Some of my favorites include the 5-minute *Give Yourself a Break* meditation, making peace with your inner critic, journaling with self-kindness, and distinguishing your own needs. As I've mentioned before, part of identifying your needs involves discerning what you are feeling first. As you do, be gentle with yourself.

GUARDING
YOUR GUT

"Quite literally, your gut is the epicenter of your mental and physical health. If you want better immunity, efficient digestion, improved clarity and balance, focus on rebuilding your gut health."

KRIS CARR

According to Dr. Jay Pasricha, Professor of Medicine and Neuroscience at Johns Hopkins School of Medicine, your gut and your brain share a special connection (via the vagus nerve) that affects how depressed or anxious you feel, how you handle stress, and how you fight off infection.

Long before experts knew about this connection, people would use the phrase "gut feeling" to describe an inkling that maybe something wasn't quite right. Today, it's not uncommon to hear those in the medical profession refer to the gut as the "second brain" because there are so many similar cells, receptors, and chemicals in the gut as in the brain. So, how do we take care of our gut health?

Eating foods such as olives, kimchi, sauerkraut, pickled vegetables or ginger, miso, kombucha, yogurt, and other fermented foods can immediately begin to increase your gut's level of good bacteria known as probiotics. And foods like lentils, chickpeas, and leeks help with a different kind of good bacteria called prebiotics.

Replacing sugar and processed foods with healthy whole foods such as vegetables, fruits, nuts, seeds, fish, olive oil, whole grains, and legumes comes with a whole plethora of benefits. According to Drew Ramsey, Assistant Clinical Professor of Psychiatry at Columbia University College of Physicians and Surgeons, these benefits include less inflammation, less depression, and improved cognitive health. A Mediterranean diet is a good place to start.

If your particular struggle has you feeling queasy, remember to eat small meals and just do the best you can. I recently learned that amino acids can help with nausea. So if you're able, try to get a little protein into your diet, even when crackers are the only food that sounds good.

STAYING WELL-WATERED

"Water is life, and clean water means health."

AUDREY HEPBURN

Many medications are anticholinergic, meaning that they block a brain chemical called acetylcholine. This can cause side effects like a dry mouth, constipation, and blurry vision. In other words, they have a dehydrating effect. This, in turn, causes our blood vessels to restrict which can make blood tests and I.V. insertions quite painful.

The normal recommendation for your daily water intake is half an ounce for every pound you weigh. So a person who weighs 150 pounds, for example, should drink 75 ounces of water each day. When taking certain medications, this is the bare minimum. A good friend of mine who has survived years of interventions related to an inherited medical condition recommended that I *really* hydrate myself any time I needed to have lab work.

So, I decided that before each monthly blood test or quarterly scan, I would drink 24 ounces of water two or three hours before I left the house. Remarkably, when I started hydrating in this way, I noticed the needle went in much more easily and was far less painful. What a wonderful recommendation!

MAINTAINING
MOBILITY

"Just keep swimming."

DORY

First of all, if your particular diagnosis involves an amputation, paralysis, muscular dystrophy, multiple sclerosis, stroke, Ehlers-Danlos syndrome, or any number of other mobility-limiting disorders, please take this next section with a grain of salt. Also, try to be open to using whatever tools you are offered such as canes, walkers, prosthetic devices, or wheelchairs to continue to propel yourself through your world as comfortably as possible.

I remember feeling so angry the first time the specialist I was seeing said that I needed to start exercising again. I semi-sarcastically mentioned "pumping iron". Didn't he care about how much pain I was experiencing? Even though he just meant walking and yoga, it didn't appear that he took any interest in how hard this would be for me. Nevertheless, I tried.

At first, despite my knowledge to the contrary, my brain had me convinced that it wouldn't be helpful at all. After being immobile for so long, I was sore and got winded so easily! Then slowly, day by day, I surprised myself by not only being able to walk a bit more, but also feeling steadier and stronger as I did. Eventually, I began to look forward to walking because it was paradoxically lessening my pain. I also enjoyed the time outdoors. The next time I met with my doctor, I gave him a heartfelt apology for my doubt. Slowly but surely, as my mobility improved, so did my mood.

FINDING
FLEXIBILITY

"I don't even have aches and pains because I started stretching."

TOM HANKS

Before delving into this section, I want to take a moment to offer it with a caveat. Obviously, you'll want to talk to your doctor about whether or not yoga is safe for you, but you might also want to check in with your own body and mind to see if it will feel safe for you at this time. If you're dealing with chronic pain, have learned to dissociate from your body, or have a history of trauma, take it slowly. Don't do too much at once. If you have a psychotherapist, it might be a good idea to talk about what it might mean for you to start or re-start a practice that involves a lot of focus on your body.

That said, if you do start slowly, you might find a bit of relief by simply stretching and paying attention to your breath.

In a small 2016 study, researcher Eric Lindahl and his team wanted to see whether a 7-week yoga program that included stretching (but not meditation) would improve perceived stress and emotional wellness in healthy elderly adults. Although participants reported little increase in physical functioning, their perceived stress and emotional well-being definitely improved. An earlier study by Jeremy West and his colleagues compared the effects of yoga to dance. They measured positive and negative mood and perceived stress in 69 college students. Interestingly, levels of the stress hormone, cortisol, fell after yoga but rose after dance, even though both groups reported feeling better overall.

For me, this was very encouraging news. Although I wasn't able to dance like I used to, I could do this... I could try some simple stretches. Indeed, yoga can be performed by just about anyone. I remember my nana, a devout Christian woman, who even in her 70s would wake up every day at 7am to do her yoga routine. It not only helped her stay fit, but also to feel good about herself. As I re-started own my yoga practice, I realized it wasn't as robust as before my diagnosis, but on the days that I did stretch, I felt much better.

HONORING
YOUR HOBBIES

"Today is life - the only life you are sure of. Make the most of today. Get interested in something. Shake yourself awake. Develop a hobby. Let the winds of enthusiasm sweep through you. Live today with gusto."

DALE CARNEGIE

There will be days when you just need a healthy distraction. Those are the times to lean into the things that bring you joy. You may have to modify your hobbies in order to continue but it's important not to fall into the trap of believing you can't enjoy yourself any longer because of your present circumstances. For example, if you love to dance like I do but have limited mobility, you can try turning on your favorite music and dancing in your chair.

Likewise, many exercises can be modified to eliminate what might cause pain or injury. I started out with chair yoga until I was finally able to get down onto the floor again. My gardening habit (or as my husband calls it, my "killing plants" habit) was initially limited to what didn't require much bending. When I decided to resume my walking routine, using the *Conqueror Challenge* virtual events as motivation, I began by simply counting the steps I walked around my backyard toward my goal. To resume my passion for cooking, I started out using an Instant Pot and elicited some help from my two favorite sous chefs, my sons!

If you love golf, perhaps try an interactive video-based golfing game. It may not feel exactly the same as before your diagnosis, but it might be just enough to help you feel a bit more like yourself again. Or if you happen to be a woodworking enthusiast like my husband, you could try building something small, like a birdhouse; easily done from your armchair or bedside table. If you enjoy crossword puzzles but your condition makes it difficult to concentrate, you might consider taking it in smaller stages. As for me, shortly after my diagnosis, I discovered the online game *Wordle* and found that a daily dose was just enough to keep my brain engaged as I healed. Whatever you choose, do it with as much gusto as you can muster, listen to your body, and take breaks when needed. This time for yourself is a precious gift.

CELEBRATING
THE SMALL
STUFF

"Celebrate good times, come on."

EUMIR DEODATO AND KOOL & THE GANG

The caring friends and family in your life will want to celebrate the big wins with you. They're looking for the illustrious positive doctor's report or the elusive yet giant physical leap forward. They want evidence that you're going to be okay so that they can also feel okay. But unless they live with you, most will not fully grasp your day-to-day experience. People who have not been through your struggle may not understand.

With that in mind, I'm here to tell you that it is really helpful to celebrate the small wins along your journey. I can remember the day I was finally able to stand up from the sofa without assistance – I definitely did my modified version of a happy dance!

So the next time you get through a meal without nausea, experience a pain-free movement, remember to take your vitamins, or are able to propel yourself around your neighborhood, take a little pause to celebrate that victory. Every little win counts!

MINDSET
MATTERS

"A positive mindset is probably the single most powerful elixir you can take for your health."

DR. CHARLES F. GLASSMAN

At some point in my journey, I had to decide that I would stubbornly refuse the role of victim and that I would rather think of myself as a victorious survivor. This wasn't a one-time reframe, though. Shifting my mindset had to happen several times along the way.

At some stage along each of our paths, we all must decide how we want to view ourselves and the world around us. But like me, you might not experience this as a simple one-time turnabout. Choosing to embrace the role of survivor or thriver may take more than one attempt. However, when we do choose to change our minds like this, the rewards can be bountiful. Here are a just few examples of how much our mindset matters.

Mindset About Abilities & Intellect

In 1999, psychologist Dr. Carol Dweck coined the terms *growth mindset* and *fixed mindset.* Here's what they mean: If a person has a fixed mindset, that individual will assume that things like intelligence, skills, and personality can't be changed. On the other hand, those with a growth mindset believe that all of these can be improved – it just takes effort – which leads to seeing obstacles or challenges as just a normal part of life and learning.

Why is this important? Having a growth mindset helps us to succeed and stay motivated. Rather than becoming discouraged when life's invariable hiccups arise, we stay the course and continue learning. On the flip side, those with a fixed mindset are more likely to either give up too soon or spend endless energy on trying to avoid challenges, simply because they believe they don't have what it takes.

Mindset About Stress

The mindset an individual chooses to adopt about stress itself is important in determining how one's body will react to stress. For example, in 2013, researchers Crum, Salovey, & Achor found that if an individual views stress as enhancing rather than dangerous, it was much healthier for that person. In other words, how we think about stress determines how we respond to stress.

Likewise, the Yerkes-Dodson law states that whereas too little or too much anxiety can be detrimental, just the right amount is actually good for us. For instance, in taking on the challenge of writing this little book, I could have said, "Meh - it'll eventually get written" and then done nothing. That's too little anxiety to be productive.

On the other hand, I could have said "This is too much! I can't do it. How can I get out of this?", which would have been too much anxiety and equally paralyzing. To be honest, I did experience a bit of each at various times. But eventually I discovered that what Yerkes-Dodson proposed is true: It really is a moderate level of anxiety that is just enough to be motivating but not so much as to be overwhelming. That balance is what kept me on the steady course toward the finish line.

Mindset About Exercise

We all feel a certain way about exercise. For many of us, it's not quite as simple as loving it or hating it. It may be more accurate to say that the relationship is "complicated". Given the research findings about stress, though, perhaps those who truly embrace exercise as a healthy, acute, life-enhancing stressor will experience the greatest performance and health-related benefits.

To test this idea, researchers Crum & Langley told 84 hotel room attendants to think of their normal daily cleaning routines as exercise. They didn't change anything else in their lifestyle other than to adopt that mindset. Remarkably, they saw significant decreases in weight, body fat, and blood pressure. It's pretty amazing to consider the powerful role mindset plays in how our bodies react!

Choosing A New Mindset

The first step to change any mindset is self-awareness - just observing your inner dialogue. What do you tell yourself about mistakes or setbacks? If you notice phrases like "I can't do this" or "I'm not good enough" coming up for you, just gently observe that these are examples of a fixed mindset.

Deliberately yet lovingly guiding yourself back to that growth-oriented frame of mind takes a conscious decision - and some effort. Remember, when you adopt a growth mindset, your internal voice is more like an optimistic encourager telling you to keep trying. You can experiment with phrases such as "I'm really having a hard time with this, but I have the tools I need," or, "Mistakes are how we learn", or my favorite, "Practice makes progress".

And finally, you can start to experiment with thinking differently about your abilities, the stress in your life, and what you *can* do to take on challenges with curiosity. You can reframe what you used to think of as a "failure" as a learning opportunity. This allows you to mentally bounce back from setbacks like the one you are facing now. The more you practice your new mindset, the more natural it will feel.

Guarding Your Mind

Each day throughout my journey, I was given a choice as to what I would allow into my brain, what I allowed myself to focus on, and what I chose to do about each situation. For example, I could fill my brain with bad news and psychological thriller films, or I could fill my brain with good news and heartwarming stories. I could choose to center my attention on all the things I was missing, or I could choose to focus on things that elicited gratitude.

Daily, I had to decide to do one small thing that I knew would help rather than choosing to do nothing and complain. Every day, I had dozens if not hundreds of opportunities to choose life, find gratitude, and fight against self-pity. Of course, all of that had to come after a period of rest. Rest feels difficult for those of us who are used to being productive, on the go, and contributing to the good of others. But rest is truly essential to healing. It was especially during that time of rest that I needed to guard my mind from negativity. Sometimes that meant avoiding conversations with well-meaning worriers; other times it meant finding creative ways to fight through the inevitable fatigue that comes from a long battle.

FIGHTING THROUGH FATIGUE

"Sometimes all it takes is a subtle shift in perspective, an opening of the mind, an intentional pause and reset, or a new route to start to see new options and new possibilities."

KRISTIN ARMSTRONG

Sometimes, you'll get through one battle only to find yourself feeling depleted and immediately forced to face another one. During such times, it may feel extra challenging to not give up on your end goal. That's the time when you might be tempted to isolate. I realized, though, that was exactly the time when I needed to invite key members of my tribe a bit closer. Stuffing my feelings and pulling away from loved ones was very unhelpful and had the potential to lead to depression.

Think about a fierce warrior out on the battlefield. Even after victory, there may be a sense of letdown, or the need to release all of that built-up tension in a way that feels emotionally safe. That's why it's important to give yourself permission to just rest or perhaps phone a safe person to process what you've experienced.

In Brené Brown's podcast episode with Amelia and Emily Nagoski on their book *Burnout*, the Nagoski twins mention seven ways that we can reset our nervous systems after we've been in fight-flight-freeze mode. Here's my personal take on how each has helped me get through the many seasons of fatigue I faced.

Exercise

Before my diagnosis, I was a dancer. Well... to be more accurate, I was a middle-aged woman who used to identify as a dancer and had morphed into enjoying the occasional Zumba class or family wedding!

For several months after my diagnosis, I simply didn't have the energy to exercise in the way I had become accustomed. My weekly routine used to involve, on average: one day of strength-training with medium weights, one day of yoga, and one day of reluctant cardio, interspersed with the occasional 5-minute dance break.

In April 2023, five months after my diagnosis, I started walking and stretching again. Let me tell you, I instantly felt a shift in my overall well-being! I was able to enjoy the sunshine, the fresh air, and more importantly, it allowed the accumulated stress in my body to escape.

Positive Social Interactions

When the weather is good, I enjoy inviting a friend over for tea. I set my outdoor table with pretty teacups and serve up snacks. When I was feeling terrible, I provided the tea and my friends provided the snacks. When it was blustery or rainy, I made Zoom coffee dates, used my Marco Polo app to send and receive short videos, or just picked up the phone to call a friend.

The Oxford Handbook of Health Psychology states that social support plays a key role in immune response, overall physical health, and even survival and longevity. It is one of the most powerful health tools we can possess. Connections can be online or in-person, and researchers note that having even just one close friend is helpful.

Social support comes in many forms. It can be emotional, such as when my friends would send me text messages or when my husband would just listen with an empathetic ear. It can be informational, such as when my friend gave me the data on various herbs to combat side effects from medicine. Or it can be in the form of what's known as "instrumental support", such as the meals I received from colleagues and church friends, or my dear neighbors taking my kiddo to band practice for the entire winter.

Deep Diaphragmatic Breathing

As I've mentioned before, belly breathing helps us to regain control after a stressful event. Researcher Susan Hopper and her team did a systematic review of several studies on the benefits of diaphragmatic breathing. They found that belly breathing does wonders for reducing stress and lowering blood pressure. And when practiced over time, it can also alleviate anxiety.

Laughing

I highly recommend finding situation comedies that are uplifting, hanging around people who are humorous, and playing games that elicit a sense of ease and fun. My husband and I enjoy British comedies, playing cards and board games with our boys, and just joking around to lighten the mood.

Research into the benefits of humor and laughter took a giant leap forward in 1964 when UCLA adjunct professor Norman Cousins was diagnosed with a painful disease and told he'd only live a few months. Cousins, you see, was a biochemistry researcher studying how emotions affect our health. He proposed that since negative emotions led to negative health outcomes, positive emotions would be healing – and he was right!

Alongside high doses of vitamin C, Cousins insisted that funny movies and laughter be part of his treatment. He experienced the immediate benefits of laughter, including pain relief and better sleep.

He also went on to live another 25 years and inspire several other researchers to discover the many laughter-related health benefits we know about today. So, find your favorite comedian, funniest television program, or silly cat videos, and laugh with abandon!

Affection

Engaging in affectionate touch doesn't have to be romantic. It can be as simple as snuggling with a pet or sharing a comforting hug with a safe friend. I have a saying, "Four hugs a day keeps the doctor away!" Even self-massage has been shown to release the bonding hormone, oxytocin, into the bloodstream. This reduces stress and increases overall well-being. So if someone to snuggle with isn't available, you can try giving yourself a hand massage or gently rubbing the back of your neck to experience similar benefits.

Crying

Remember that warrior? What if after the battle, that person felt safe enough to lay down their sword and shield to cry and release all the built-up tension? Can you imagine how healing that would be if all of us did that? Unfortunately, many either expect crying to make them feel worse or else judge themselves for not being "strong" enough.

Although the research is mixed, many who choose to allow their tears to flow following a stressful event tend to report feeling better after a good cry. When I have chosen to view the intentional releasing of my tears as good for me, or simply used the phrase "I give myself permission", I've felt notably better than when I've engaged in negative self-talk either about crying or during a cry.

Creative Expression

Once I started to feel a bit better, I decided to bring out an old scrapbooking project I hadn't gotten around to finishing. Minutes would tick by seemingly unnoticed. The same would happen while reading an intriguing novel set in a different place and time. I would absolutely lose myself in a lovely way! When we engage with life in an artistic manner by journaling, dancing, cooking, drawing, painting, reading, crafting, creating, or writing, we can enter a state of flow.

Flow is where you lose track of time because you are so pleasantly focused on the creative task at hand that everything else seems to disappear. In flow, stress hormones dissipate and a sense of well-being ensues. So even if you don't consider yourself artistic, you may find that mindfully doing something creative is another great way to release the stress that is stored in your body.

MELTING INTO MINDFULNESS

"The present moment holds infinite riches beyond your wildest dreams, but you will only enjoy them to the extent of your faith and love."

JEAN-PIERRE DE CAUSSADE

Mindfulness may be one of the most misunderstood practices I recommend to my clients. While some imagine it must take great effort, others assume they must empty their minds and potentially allow something bad to enter. According to John Kabat-Zinn, founder of Mindfulness Based Stress Reduction (MBSR), mindfulness simply involves "paying attention, on purpose, in the present moment, non-judgmentally".

Mindfulness has been researched extensively

as a low-risk, easy-to-develop habit that is often used as a component of treatment for depression, anxiety, chronic pain, and cardiac health. Here's how it works:

The part of the brain responsible for detecting threats and responding with anger or fear is called the amygdala. Brain scans show that after people learn mindfulness, their amygdala is less activated. In other words, mindfulness quite literally taught their brains how to calm themselves down. Below are a few ways you can incorporate mindfulness into your own life.

Delay Deciding

As you experience each of your daily activities, see if you can suspend judgment. Experiment with the idea of just letting things be as they are, without deciding anything about them. Simply notice what is.

Inhale Intentionally

A good place to begin is by inhaling through your nose and feeling the coolness of the air as it enters your nostrils. Then shift your attention to how your belly and side body expand as your lungs fill with air. When you exhale, you may choose to open your mouth, blowing all of the air out until your body naturally signals that it needs another breath.

After practicing for a number of years, I've noticed that repeating this just three or four times lowers my heart rate and instantly helps to calm me down in moments when I've needed it most.

Feel Something Fluffy

Whether it's the fur of your favorite pet, a snuggly blanket, or the grass between your toes, take some time to feel the sensation of something soft. Soft textures tend to be very calming and help us regulate our emotions.

Move Mindfully

When you head outdoors, if you are able, try to pay attention to how your feet touch the surface beneath you, how your arms swing beside you, the sensation of the air, and whether it is cool or warm. See if you can synchronize your steps with your breath.

Notice Nature

Whether you're at the beach, exploring your neighborhood, or even in the comfort of your own home, look up and notice your surroundings. What colors do you see? Do you hear the sounds of birds or cars or people? Just take note of it without evaluation.

Simply Smell

The next time you're making your morning coffee or tea, see if you can pause for a moment to enjoy the wafting scent of the coffee beans or tea leaves. Close your eyes and inhaling deeply. Then again, before you take that first sip, wrap your hands around the warm cup and breathe deeply.

Truly Taste

Before tasting a piece of chocolate or biting into an orange, stop and notice. How does it feel in your hand? Does the smell make you salivate? As you take a bite, let it linger in your mouth for a while before you begin to chew. As you swallow, notice how this feels also.

There are many other ways to experience the present moment without judging it. Have fun experimenting with mindfulness and incorporating it into your daily routine. As you do, you may notice that you develop more patience, an increased ability to regulate your reactions, a better sense of well-being, and more resilience to handle your difficult circumstances.

A RECIPE FOR RELAXATION

> *"Each person deserves a day away in which no problems are confronted, no solutions searched for. Each of us needs to withdraw from the cares which will not withdraw from us."*

MAYA ANGELOU

In my kitchen, I have a page torn from an old magazine that talks about the best way to create an excellent salad. The author recommends adding to your favorite greens the following: some type of fruit, some type of nut, and some type of cheese. It's a recipe for salad success I've used time and time again.

Recently, while making a salad, I was struck again by the recommendations in the Nagoski twins' book *Burnout* of all the ways to complete the stress cycle. I realized that if I engage in self-care practices regularly, my body wouldn't have to remain in a state of frazzle and frustration. And so I began to ponder these recommendations in a different way.

Between these two ideas (completing the stress cycle and creating the perfect salad), it got me thinking: What if I could create a recipe for a self-care plan that was sustainable enough to get through the long-haul? Perhaps it would look something like this:

Start With Spirituality

Whether it's a morning meditation or an evening reading plan, find a daily practice that connects you with the divine. This will allow you to touch base with what's truly important to you. Connecting with your tribe for a combined spiritual practice can be especially powerful and mutually encouraging.

Embrace What's Energizing

What's most rejuvenating to you? What brings you joy? Is it a particular hobby or volunteer project? Perhaps it's spending time with certain people or in a particular place. Do what makes you feel alive again!

Add Activity

This could be anything from walking to weeding, from swimming to sit-ups, from yoga to yodeling (okay, maybe not yodeling, but you get the idea). In whatever capacity you are able, find a fun way to be active!

Cap It Off With Creativity

I talked about this a bit before but it bears repeating. Don't give up on what brings you joy! You may like cooking or crafts, poetry or painting, making music or merely puttering with a handy DIY project. Whatever you choose, allow yourself some space to enjoy the process.

Allow yourself to become fully immersed in a creative activity so you can enjoy that state of flow. You can also think of this as feeling "in the zone" or being "in the pocket". Just focus exclusively on the pleasurable task at hand - it's healthy for both your body and your brain.

Putting It All Together

Like any good recipe, it's how you put it all together that makes the difference. Some recipes, like this one, can be varied. Try to choose something from each category every week that doesn't feel like a chore and is affordable enough to sustain.

Just remember, the goal is consistent rest and rejuvenation. If it's too expensive or complex, you'll be less likely to continue any self-care practice. But if you can find affordable ways to "refill your teapot", then you can create your own recipe that will go the distance.

UNWINDING WORRY

"Worrying is carrying tomorrow's load with today's strength - carrying two days at once. It is moving into tomorrow ahead of time. Worrying doesn't empty tomorrow of its sorrow, it empties today of its strength."

CORRIE TEN BOOM

My husband and I recently had a conversation about the differences between anxiety and worry. I proposed that worry tends to be more specific than anxiety. There are several things you might choose to worry about every day, especially when you are dealing with all of the uncertainties of your current health issues. But worry actually ends up having the opposite effect of what you hope.

In fact, it can make your health worse rather than better. So why do people do this? If we can figure out *why* we do it, it may help us to choose better coping skills. Here are a few of the main reasons we humans worry:

Always On Alert

There are two types of anxiety: short-term state anxiety and chronic trait anxiety. State anxiety is a temporary psychological and physiological reaction to a stressful situation. It's actually pretty adaptive. On the other hand, trait anxiety is more of an always-on-alert condition that, if left untreated, can lead to some not-so-healthy conditions.

But before you heap self-criticism on top of trait anxiety, it's important to know that this chronic fear response may have started off as its more adaptive counterpart during times of trauma. I personally think it's chronic anxiety that feeds the "worry monster", but it's also important to recognize that both kinds of anxiety are treatable.

Busy Brain

Our brains are always "on", even when we're asleep. During the daytime, our "little grey cells" are analyzing and problem-solving, learning and remembering, planning and implementing. It's nonstop! Even at night when we curl up in bed, our brains are integrating all that we've learned and experienced throughout the day.

Sleep is also supposed to be a time for rest and repair, which is why it's important to engage in something relaxing before bedtime, such as reading or meditating.

Conflation Or Confusion

Worry tricks our brains into feeling like we're doing something productive. When we engage in the "What if..." game, it seems like we're doing ourselves a favor. It's as if we can ward off any impending negative circumstances by devoting time and energy to concentrating on them.

Sometimes, we combine what we know about problem solving with the unhealthy belief that trying to prepare for every possible negative outcome is somehow helpful, even though we know from experience that we can't predict the future and that worrying just increases our distress. Rather than finding joy or gratitude in the present moment, we make ourselves miserable by constantly searching for danger around every corner. It can get really exhausting!

So how do we rest, repair, or even just relax when some of us tend towards constant high alert and others just don't know what to do instead? Here are a few ideas:

Calm the Curiosity

In the world of psychology, there's a skill that we call "tolerance of ambiguity". It's the ability to calmly deal with the unknown. None of us can predict what tomorrow will bring and very few uncertain situations actually turn out to be as dangerous or threatening as we imagine. Rather than losing sleep, you can try this experiment: First, write down in one column what you believe about knowing versus not knowing. For example, "I believe that not knowing is dangerous and knowing will keep me safe". In a second column, describe what coping technique you used the last time something triggered this belief. For example, "The last time I felt this way, I used deep breathing and pleasant activities to calm and distract myself until I the information arrived in due course". In a third column, purposely create a situation where you don't know the outcome and write it down. In a fourth column, write down what actually happened. And finally, compare what actually happened to what you expected. The more you practice this, the more your tolerance will grow.

Lovingly List

Before going to bed, if you're concerned about

the things you must accomplish the next day, you could try very briefly jotting down a quick to-do list and let that part of your brain take the night off. Be careful not to lapse into anxious self-talk. By keeping it simple and straightforward, as if you're making a grocery list, you may notice yourself drifting off to sleep afterwards more easily.

Worry During a Window

Here's how this works: Set an alarm for the same time each day. During this time, write down every single anxious thought you can for a full 15 minutes. If you find yourself starting to worry outside of this window, just remind yourself in a very gentle way, "Thank you, brain, for trying to keep me safe. We'll write this down during the Worry Window. Until then, we can set this aside."

You may even find yourself pleasantly surprised. Some who practiced this for several days or weeks have noticed that when their Worry Time came around, many of the things they previously found perturbing either weren't important enough to include or better yet, that they couldn't even remember what they were supposed to worry about. Now wouldn't that be lovely?

ALLEVIATING ANXIETY

*"The beginning of anxiety is the end of faith, and
the beginning of true faith is the end of anxiety."*

GEORGE MUELLER

Do you ever get so stuck in your head that
it feels like you can't move? Do you find yourself
ruminating over things you think might happen?
Sometimes you may feel like you already know the
outcome, but do you really? Or perhaps, that if you
can just avoid that one thing, then everything will
be alright. But is avoidance helpful?

Avoidance plays a negative role in a number
of mental health issues, and it usually begins with
self-talk. I have a saying: "Anxiety eats avoidance for
breakfast". In other words, if you're anxious about
something and you do everything in your power to

avoid that something, then the anxiety will actually grow stronger and stronger every time you avoid it. Avoidance feeds the anxiety.

For example, let's say that you're nervous about pigeons. You might have a very good reason for this – maybe one pooped on your head when you were a small child, or perhaps one pecked at your toes and it frightened you. So now, you avoid pigeons. At first glance, that might seem like a logical solution. But every time you avoid a pigeon, you train your brain to believe that pigeons are dangerous. Eventually, you may begin to generalize this to all birds. If this pattern continues, your world may start to feel very small because you will begin to avoid any place that pigeons even *might* visit.

To counteract this fear-based instinct, you could try starting with the small step of just looking at pigeons online. Then you might follow up with a trip to visit a local park where pigeons sometimes gather. Eventually, you may feel comfortable expanding your world to include several areas where birds might visit, which would lead to a greater sense of freedom - rather than fear.

Fear is an insidious enemy. Some have developed an acronym for fear: False Evidence Appearing Real. This certainly seems like an accurate description. Fear will feed you a pack of lies and anxiety frequently predicts the future to be far worse than it actually ends up being.

When I was in fifth grade, I was on the blacktop playing basketball during P.E. class. One of the bigger kids passed the ball to me and instead of catching it, I got hit right in the stomach. I was a very thin child, so this basketball was big compared to me! The next thing I knew, I was flat on my back, desperately trying to gasp for air, but completely unable to catch my breath. I'd gotten the wind knocked out of me. That's what acute anxiety feels like. When you first receive a difficult diagnosis, or get that phone call you never wanted, or experience any type of terrible trauma, it's like getting the wind knocked out of you.

This feeling is similar to a short-term, immediate, and adaptive anxiety response, such as you might experience while being chased by a bear. This is totally normal. It prompts you to take action. But long-term anxiety is not your friend. When bouts of unhealthy anxiety strike, it's important to disrupt the avoidance tendency like I've described here. In addition, I have a veritable tool box of calming practices that I use. The first step for me is to get control of my breath.

BREATHING FROM YOUR BELLY

"Breathe like you mean it."

JOHN LANDRY

The diaphragm is a dome-shaped muscle located directly below your lungs. Its job is to help you breathe more efficiently. Babies instinctively breathe from their bellies. But as we get older, and allow anxiety to take over, we sometimes find ourselves taking shorter, shallower breaths from our chests. Occasionally, I've even noticed myself holding my breath!

Diaphragmatic breathing, also known as belly breathing, reverses this and helps us to calm down and almost instantly start breathing more efficiently. I've mentioned the benefits of deep breathing already. So, here are the steps to get the most out of it:

First of all, simply imagine that your lungs are like balloons. Next, place one hand on your belly and the other on your chest. Your goal will be to allow the bottom hand to rise and fall naturally with each breath while keeping the top hand on your chest relatively still. To inflate your lungs, breathe in through your nose, allowing your belly to inflate as you do. As you breathe out, either through your nose or mouth, you will notice that your belly automatically falls, like a balloon that is being deflated. Repeat this process until it feels natural.

If you find this practice difficult to do while sitting up, you can start by lying down. When I first began this practice, I discovered it was helpful to place a piece of paper on my belly so I could see the natural rise and fall of my breath more easily. Once I got the hang of it, I was able to practice this way of deep breathing while sitting in a relaxed position.

It's easy to take breathing for granted. But when we choose to bring our attention to this autonomic process, it allows us to slow down, calm down, and proverbially feel our feet on the ground again - even in the midst of trying circumstances.

GETTING GROUNDED

*"Get yourself grounded and you can navigate
even the stormiest roads in peace."*

STEVE GOODIER

Have you ever tried to relax, only to find yourself feeling more stressed or even triggered in the process? If this happens to you, you may want to try grounding instead. Grounding techniques are a bit different from relaxation strategies, in that they are designed to bring your attention to the present moment. This is especially important if you're stuck thinking of something that happened in the past, or worrying about some unknown future event.

If you incorporate an element of something you find spiritually healing as well, grounding can be a powerful way to remind yourself that you're safe even amidst difficult circumstances. Here are a few I've found helpful:

Aromatherapy

Experiment with different essential oils or fragranced lotions to find which ones make you feel most relaxed. I personally like lavender and frankincense.

Create Art

Drawing, painting, or coloring helps you enter the state of flow discussed earlier, which is very soothing. You can even draw a place you find safe and calming.

Do a Mental Puzzle

Try counting and matching at the same time, such as 1-A, 2-B, etc. This uses both sides of your brain, and helps you focus.

Feel Textures

Compare different textures like a soft fabric or a hard, smooth stone to engage your sense of touch as you explore what is present with you.

Go Shoeless

Get grounded in a more literal sense by standing barefoot in some cool grass.

Go for a Walk

Walking, especially in nature, releases endorphins

and enhances clarity. Mindfully observe your environment.

Grab a Grounding Object

Keep a small object in your pocket. This could be anything meaningful that reminds you you're strong, safe, and loved.

Mindful Eating

Try biting into a slice of lemon or tangerine. Notice the scent, texture, and finally the flavor. Doing so will keep you present.

Pet an Animal

Petting a cat, dog, rabbit, horse, or other furry friend can quickly lower anxiety.

Rainbow Colors

Look around you and see if you can find one object in every color of the rainbow: red, orange, yellow, green, blue, indigo, and violet.

Run Your Hands Under Water

Warm water tends to relax; cold water makes you feel alert - especially if you splash it on your face!

Sing or Hum a Favorite Song

Choose a tune that you find calming or reassuring. This could be an uplifting song from any genre, so long as it helps you stay in the here-and-now.

Smile

Even if it's hard, try putting yourself in a 60-second "smiling time-out". You may even find yourself laughing, which is good medicine. It boosts immunity, relaxes muscles, and relieves pain.

Stretch

Reach up to the sky; then let your body hang loosely over your feet; stretch your fingers and toes; hunch your shoulders and then let them drop down again. Repeat as often as needed.

The next time you find yourself focusing on the past or feeling distressed about the future, try one of these grounding techniques to bring you back to the present moment. It may aid you in remembering that you're safe, help you to stay calm, and connect you to your surroundings.

REELING IN
"REALISM"

"When you get into a tight place and everything goes against you, till it seems as though you could not hang on a minute longer, never give up then, for that is just the place and time that the tide will turn."

HARRIET BEECHER STOWE

Every pessimist I've ever met is a self-described "realist". I often hear that it's better to expect the worst than to hope for something good and be disappointed. So it would seem that having a "glass-half-empty" mentality would be good for us, right? Actually, according to a ten-year University of Michigan study with over 21,000 participants, the exact opposite is true. Even when controlling for other factors, researchers noted that optimism had a significant effect on longevity, along with purpose, social support, and positive affect. Another study, conducted at The Rockefeller Center in New York, found that optimism was associated with "exceptional longevity". They also noted that more optimistic individuals took better care of themselves.

When I was in college, I was introduced to the concept of positive psychology. I was encouraged when I discovered that the main tenets were in line with my own personal belief system. I then explored several fascinating articles from UC Berkeley's Greater Good Science Center that helped to provide further scientific backing for what I already surmised to be true. The focus on love, joy, compassion, altruism, resilience, spirituality, the mind-body connection, and hope were all linked in some way or another to overall well-being.

So, what docs all of this optimism and positivity have to do with getting through the rough time you're experiencing right now? If you're looking forward with hope, and are feeling positive about your treatment plan, you're more likely to not only survive, but thrive! That doesn't mean that true realism is bad. It just means that we need to look at it in a more balanced way.

I came to understand what healthy realism looks like while perusing The A.R.T. of Survival reading plan by Chip Ingram. In it, he talks about prisoners of war who gave up versus those who made it through until their release. The difference, Ingram noted, was in their attitude. Those who were overly optimistic as to the specific *timing* of their release tended to become more disappointed as time progressed and they eventually gave up. On the other hand, those who were able to mentally prepare themselves to persevere through the tough times were the ones who survived to see their hope realized.

Finding this balance between holding hope and staying strong during the tough times was a challenge that took some deliberate effort for me to master. In doing so, I discovered that the richness of remaining confidently expectant combined with the groundedness of being authentically pragmatic helped me to stay motivated for the long haul.

PONDERING
THE PARADOX

"Surfing isn't the most important thing in life. Love is. I've had the chance to embrace more people with one arm than I ever could with two."

BETHANY HAMILTON

In times of suffering like you and I have endured, many people report feelings of gratitude, an epiphany about what really matters, and a persistent sense of meaning, joy, or peace that is different from any other time in their lives. For me personally, I experienced an unshakeable faith, unrelenting hope, and an inexplicable sense of spirituality that was like never before.

While encouraging me to write this book, my neighbor advised that I talk about "God's upside-down kingdom". For those who know, you know. For those who aren't familiar with this term, it's hard to describe, but I'll give it a try.

In the Disney Pixar movie, *Cars,* Doc Hudson tries to explain to Lightning McQueen how to navigate a particularly tricky turn on a dirt track. Quite the hotshot, McQueen thought he knew what he was doing. So, when Hudson gives him sound but unexpected advice, McQueen responds with, "Oh, right. That makes perfect sense. Turn *right* to go *left.* Yes, thank you! Or should I say No, thank you, because in Opposite World, maybe that really means thank you." You see, McQueen was used to driving on paved racetracks. Of course, he crashes when he tries to do it his way, but when he heeds Hudson's words of wisdom, it paradoxically turns out well for him (pun intended).

Recently, my family and I discovered a television series called *The Chosen.* In it, there's a ragtag group of young Middle Eastern men who each end up meeting a man who does things in a really paradoxical way. He tends to value the people who society scorns, advise things that are seemingly absurd (like doing good to people who hate you), and seems perfectly content to travel around with very little wordly possessions. Yet somehow, by following this guy, they all eventually find themselves experiencing more meaning, purpose, wholeness, and well-being.

This man was Jesus. Even if you aren't interested in Christianity, per se, *The Chosen* is a very well-made program. If you are interested in learning more, or if you want something even more historically accurate, I recommend an app called YouVersion. Ever since my diagnosis, I've found myself more emboldened to share my faith; not in a cram-it-down-your-throat sort of way, but just inviting people to get curious. I can't imagine enduring all I've gone through during the past year without the most important relationship in my life.

In the upside-down kingdom of God, things happen in unexpected ways. Peace occurs in the midst of turmoil. Being forgiven leads to the ability to forgive. In weakness, strength is found. And true joy is experienced despite suffering.

EXPECTING THE UNEXPECTED

"When we lose one blessing, another is often most unexpectedly given in its place."

C.S. LEWIS

A week before my diagnosis, I went to my eye doctor to pick up my new glasses. Somehow, the lab accidentally made a pair of reading glasses for me rather than driving glasses. I set them aside, thinking that I would have this "error" corrected later. What I didn't know was that over the next few months, I wouldn't be able to drive. I would actually need those beautiful blue reading glasses instead! God was providing for me even before I knew what I needed.

In addition to my reading glasses, I noticed many other unexpected blessings during the first several weeks after my diagnosis. I think of these as "mini miracles". For example, one evening my family ordered groceries to be delivered the following day. When nothing arrived, I contacted the grocery store to see what had happened. They recommended I look around to see if anyone in our neighborhood might have accidentally received them. My youngest son looked and didn't see any groceries on anyone's front porch, so the store replaced our order. A couple of days later, our next door neighbors returned from a couple's getaway vacation and realized our groceries were delivered to their home instead (their son had brought them into the house and didn't tell anyone). So we got double groceries!

Another example is how my husband and I had saved up and were thinking of purchasing a car but had decided a few weeks before my diagnosis to hold off on that decision, leaving the money in the bank. Other financial blessings kept coming as well. We found thousands of unused dollars on our health savings card; my husband's bonus was exactly the amount we needed to cover medical expenses; friends gave us gift cards or brought us meals when I couldn't cook; the list goes on!

I considered even the fact that our leaves changed colors late in the season as a mini-miracle also. When I was at my weakest, I could lie on our sofa and look out at the beautiful fall colors and marvel at God's provision for me. I think the most miraculous moment, though, was one that happened on a night shortly after I began treatment for my condition. My husband had gone out to pick up dinner and I noticed my hand quickly becoming swollen and discolored, a sign of a potentially dangerous side effect from the medication I had just started taking. My oldest son was sitting across the room from me, witnessing the whole event. I started praying fervently for healing and within moments, the dark spots and swelling had completely disappeared. My son and I were so amazed!

Months later, when I was contemplating what it would mean to return to work, I was assured that I could start slowly with fewer clients. This meant that I would be able to continue to earn hours, receive supervision and training, and not have to overstress my body. This was another huge, unexpected blessing. My gratitude for the ongoing care and support I've received from my management team and colleagues is inexpressible.

If there is anything this journey has taught me, it is to expect the unexpected. Throughout the first several months of my illness, I frequently would say, "God can heal me as quickly or as slowly as He wants", knowing that there would be some purpose in either. That doesn't mean the waiting was always easy, though.

WAITING WELL

"Waiting is a period of learning. The longer we wait, the more we hear about him for whom we are waiting."

HENRI NOUWEN

Each year for nearly a decade, I have chosen a Word of the Year for myself. I replaced my annual tradition of writing New Year's Resolutions (that I usually broke by the end of January!) with a single word to bear in mind throughout the year. Over the years, my words have included: Balance, Gratitude, Hope, Focus, Shine, Joy, Peace, Rejuvenate, and Light. I have found that keeping a single word or phrase in mind to be a much gentler way to keep myself on track with what I value.

In early autumn of 2022, I had already started contemplating the words Pause or Rest for 2023. Having survived a seemingly never-end pandemic with an inherited medical condition, this seemed appropriate. Even while I was counseling my clients to take good care of themselves, I knew that I myself was doing too much and ignoring my body. I was planning to *eventually* see my primary care physician for a checkup. Little did I know how much I would need that rest, how life-threatening my diagnosis would be, and how literal that pause was to become.

In Magnolia magazine, television star Joanna Gaines writes in her article entitled Worth the Weight, "I'm learning that we can have all sorts of endings but we all arrive there as a different version of ourselves based on how we hold the middle." She goes on to state, "It's not a passive kind of pause but an active awareness of the weight it carries".

About midway through my recovery, I met a lab tech who encouraged me to write about waiting in hope. This was one of the most challenging aspects of my difficult time, especially when God seemed quiet. All throughout my life, whenever someone would remind me that "patience is a virtue...", I would quickly tack on "... one I do not possess". So, it took a definitive act of will to, once again, be open to the ideas in the following Bible passage from Romans 5:

"Therefore, since we have been justified by faith, we have peace with God through our Lord

Jesus Christ. Through him we have also obtained access by faith into this grace in which we stand, and we rejoice in hope of the glory of God. Not only that, but we rejoice in our sufferings, knowing that suffering produces endurance, and endurance produces character, and character produces hope, and hope does not put us to shame, because God's love has been poured into our hearts through the Holy Spirit who has been given to us".

Okay, now, I'm the first to admit that the idea of having access to God is way easier to accept than the idea of suffering producing anything good. I spent my whole life trying to *avoid* suffering, often not successfully. However, I think there are different ways to deal with suffering. For example, a 2021 research team led by Dr. Sarah Pressman found that people who smiled while receiving an injection reported about 40% less pain. There is an undeniable mind-body connection that makes rejoicing in suffering seem a bit more plausible.

Yes, believers in Christ have hope because there's access to God's throne of grace; we can also have hope even in the midst of trying times. It's a classic case of what I call 'both-and'. When it seemed like God was silent, I needed to focus on three things to reset my perspective:

First of all, I had to remind myself that God is good. Humans have gotten into all kinds of trouble by believing the opposite, starting with Adam and Eve. Secondly, I had to remind myself of God's unfailing love. Just because I was going through a tough time didn't mean God lost his love for me. And finally, it was very helpful to go back and revisit the times that God has shown up for me in some beautiful and amazing ways; to remember other miracles both big and small. That realization made the waiting much more tolerable.

When I first received my diagnosis, I asked my physician what caused it. He was quick to state we shouldn't "blame the victim". Some people might instead turn to blaming God. I knew that this wouldn't be good for me. My condition was merely a byproduct of living in a broken and fallen world. God was there, right by my side, helping me through each step of my journey.

DECIDING TO BE DIFFERENT

"Focusing on the negative only makes a difficult journey more difficult."

TOBYMAC

When you are on the other side of your current circumstance, you will be different in many ways. Some of those ways will simply be physical results of what you've endured. In other ways, you can choose to be different, even during the journey. You can be intentional on how you want that to look for you personally, beginning now.

Elizabeth Barrett Browning was a 17th-century English poet who suffered for years with mysterious illnesses. Modern physicians hypothesize she had some form of encephalomyelitis (inflammation of the central nervous system that damages the protective myelin that insulates nerve fibers) resulting from an injury she sustained from a kick by her pony. After years in isolation, she wrote a poem entitled "Cheerfulness Taught by Reason" which begins:

> "I think we are too ready with complaint.
> In this fair world of God's."

It is difficult for able-bodied, healthy individuals to fathom the discomfort and pain that some of us have to endure on our road to recovery. Nonetheless, I have found that the narrative in my own mind is truly powerful. It can aid in the healing, or it can make me even more miserable when I am already suffering. Why do we do this? I suspect it is because we want – like all humans – to be understood and validated. When we are not, we weave an intricate story in our heads, detailing every last problem. But does this help? I think it does not. After years of suffering alone, Elizabeth chose to adopt a different mindset that allowed her to re-engage in life, and this eventually led to her meeting and marrying fellow poet Robert Browning. Just as she resolved to be different, so can we.

It all starts with deciding what kind of legacy you'd like to leave. How do you want to be known? What wisdom or gift or idea do you want to impart to others? It's also tremendously important to view that negative narrative in your head as your enemy and not your friend. Whenever I found myself spiraling down into those dark thoughts, I'd simply picture a stop sign and tell myself, "Stop. Just stop. This isn't helping right now." Then I would replace those thoughts with more adaptive, hopeful beliefs.

So how am I different today? I would like to think that after this season, I am getting better at being more patient, and less critical of myself and others. I am also extremely grateful for this life of mine, however long it may last. In that, I give myself permission to feel loved, to experience joy, and to make time for what's important.

But I know that without a tremendous amount of continual mental and spiritual effort to pursue a humble attitude daily, all of these changes - all of my lessons learned - could be temporary. Again, this is where seeking honest feedback from trusted tribe members has been instrumental for me to keep growing.

LIVING OUT
THE LESSONS

"There is nothing like returning to a place that remains unchanged to find the ways in which you yourself have altered."

NELSON MANDELA

I want to preface this next section by saying that I don't think my diagnosis was God's way of punishing me. That said, I do believe that there are lessons to be learned in every trial; in every struggle. Your lessons learned are sure to be different from mine. For me, one of the main lessons has been finding ways to hone my humility.

I had been so arrogant about living a healthy lifestyle that I failed to get timely check-ups. I was also prideful in other areas of my life and it came out sideways. I remember a conversation I had with someone who lovingly pointed this out in me shortly before my diagnosis. It was so clear in the moment that she was right – I had nothing to say in my own defense and I knew I needed to change.

Needless to say, I found myself with time on my hands to really pursue this notion of pulverizing my pride. So, I found a wonderful book series by Elisabeth Bennett written for each number on the Enneagram, a model of nine different yet interconnected personality types. The book I chose was written for those who identify, like me, as an Enneagram 2 (the Helper). In it, I found the same loving tone, which made it easier to confront the prideful part of myself. I was able to look back over my career as well as my personal life and recognize that it was exactly the times in which I embraced true humility that I was able to learn the most from others. But what is true humility?

In *Mere Christianity,* author C.S. Lewis describes a man who was truly humble. What made this person truly humble in Lewis' opinion is that the man was not thinking of himself as humble, but rather that he wasn't thinking of himself at all. Knowing that I didn't have to trade in my sense of worth for humility, I made it my goal to "ask; not tell".

The result was that I reopened myself to having others speak wisdom into my life; wisdom which has proved immensely valuable. Many times my friends, colleagues, and even the people I am mentoring or counseling will have more knowledge, wisdom, or faith than me. That's not only okay, it's wonderful! Learning is a two-way street.

INVESTIGATING INTERCESSORY PRAYER

"Prayer is to the skeptic a delusion, a waste of time. To the believer it represents perhaps the most important use of time."

PHILIP YANCEY

Because healing prayer often does not fit within the traditional medical model, the scientific literature is somewhat lacking. Yet even within studies trying to disprove its efficacy, we see hope. In 2000, a mind-body researcher, Dr. John Astin and his colleagues published a review of 23 studies in the Annals of Internal Medicine to evaluate distance healing interventions, such as intercessory prayer. In the majority of cases, they found statistically significant positive effects.

From 2015 to 2020, a team at the Amsterdam University Medical Center evaluated 27 claims of healing by prayer and found 11 to be medically remarkable, instantaneous, and transformative.

In 2016, researchers from Duke University Medical Center and the Houston V.A. Center teamed up with researchers from Saudi Arabia to evaluate the effects of healing prayer on patients with depression. They discovered that 11 of 14 improved significantly, and results were still evident at the patients' 12-month follow-up appointments.

In 2021, my husband and I took a class on how to pray from an organization called Novo. In this class, we learned about listening prayer, blessing others, physical healing and inner healing prayer, and so forth. Although the evidence was not scientifically evaluated, there were many reports shared of healing and other positive changes noted by participants.

Some of my clients over the years have been Christians; some practice other religions; still others don't associate with any particular faith. As a Christian therapist, I have made space for all to simply show up. I meet them right where they are and incorporate as much or as little spiritual exploration as they desire.

That said, I do espouse a deep faith within my

own life. I have found prayer to be helpful during challenging circumstances, like my most recent one, wherein I have experienced truly profound - dare I say miraculous - healing.

FINDING
YOUR FAITH

"Faith is not believing in my own unshakable belief. Faith is believing an unshakable God when everything in me trembles and quakes."

BETH MOORE

People have varying definitions of what faith means. Some think of faith as a religious tradition, as in "What faith are you?". Others think of it as a sort of stick-to-it attitude, such as "Keep the faith". Still others may be convinced that faith can only be truly experienced inside a particular building or on a certain day of the week.

I think of faith like this: I say that my chair can support me. Then I actually sit down in it. That's faith. It's a sort of trust that prompts me to take action in some instances and to wait patiently in others.

The Bible defines faith as "the assurance of things hoped for, the evidence of things not seen" (Hebrews 11:1), and then goes on to give several examples of individuals who exhibited great faith. Some of these people waited years to see God's promises to them fulfilled and others stepped out and experienced seemingly impossible things because they believed.

Faith and hope have been inextricably linked in my own journey. It meant that I stubbornly refused to give up on the thought that God would heal me in his own time. Some days were harder than others but I always came back to reminding myself of God's character.

Sometimes well-meaning family and friends will say that all religions are the same. Over the years, I have discovered there are basically two kinds of religions in the world. The first kind is more popular. It's based on the same principle that makes us fight against someone buying us lunch. We want to either do the paying or pay them back. This type of religion teaches that if I work hard enough, do all the right things, and say the right words enough times, then somehow I can make myself acceptable to God.

The second type is less of a religion and more of a relationship. It's the type of relationship where one is perfect (God) and the other is not (me). God knows that I, being the imperfect one, can never do enough to become perfect on my own. In that knowledge, he offers me grace.

I know that my future, both now and forever, is secure because of this grace. I rest in that faith knowing that any good deeds I do are merely out of gratitude because I am already forgiven. I have direct access to my Father God. I don't have to go through a priest or pundit. I don't have to live a thousand lives trying to get it right. I am thankful for this gift of grace, and I am especially thankful for this kind of relationship.

GIVING SPACE
FOR GOD

"The God of the Bible is also the God of the genome. He can be worshipped in the cathedral or in the laboratory. His creation is majestic, awesome, intricate and beautiful - and it cannot be at war with itself."

DR. FRANCIS S. COLLINS

Ask ten different people who or what they think God is, and you're likely to receive ten different answers. Or some will say that they cannot believe in God at all because they believe in science. After thoughtful consideration, I realized that science was never intended to be a belief system. The scientific method is merely a means of finding out what is already true. Therefore, scientific thinking and faith in a divine creator can coexist.

My go-to textbook on spiritual matters is the Bible. Yours may be the Torah or the Qur'an or the Guru Granth Sahib or the Bhagavad Gita or the writings of Buddha. Or perhaps you're one of the people, scientific or not, who's never given much thought to the existence of God.

Allow me to share a few names of God found in the Jewish Tanakh (the Old Testament of the Bible) that I believe reveal His character:

Elohim: The Living God
El Shaddai: Lord God Almighty
El Roi: The God Who Sees Me
Adonai: Lord, Master
Yehowah/Jehovah/Yaweh: The Self-Existent One
Jehovah-Jireh: The Lord Who Provides
Jehovah-Shalom: The Lord My Peace
Jehovah-Raah: The Lord My Shepherd
Jehovah-Rapha: The Lord Who Heals
Jehovah-Shammah: The Lord is There

During my darkest times, I found contemplating God's promises to his people to be very comforting. There are literally hundreds of promises in the Bible. Here I have listed just a handful that are particularly meaningful to me. God promises: care (I Peter 5:7), comfort (II Corinthians 1:3-4), compassion (Psalm 116:5-6), and faithfulness (Psalm 9:10, Isaiah 25:1, I Thessalonians 5:24). He also promises that he hears us (Psalm 10:17; 34:17) and to bring good out of suffering (II Corinthians 4:17, Galatians 6:9, Romans 8:28, Isaiah 61:1-3).

We are also assured that God is good (Psalm 27:13, Psalm 119:68, James 1:17), that he gives guidance to those who seek it (Psalm 32:8, Proverbs 3:5-6), that he offers hope (Jeremiah 29:11, Hebrews 6:19-20), and that he is the very definition of love (I John 4:8, Psalm 103:17). Not only that, but those who trust in the Lord are also offered inexplicable peace (Isaiah 26:3, Philippians 4:7), joy that isn't dependent on circumstance (Psalm 126:5-6, Psalm 94:19), and the strength to get through tremendous difficulties (Psalm 46:1, Philippians 4:11-13). And perhaps most importantly, during what feels like our loneliest times, God promises to be with us (Psalm 34:18, James 4:8, John 14:23, Hebrews 13:5).

I think I have struggled the most in my life when I have forgotten one or more of these attributes of my loving Father. Just like Adam and Eve who had everything they needed in the Garden of Eden but doubted his goodness, when I have chosen to believe that God isn't good and loving, it has increased my suffering. When I remember all the ways he's come through for me, that he can be trusted, and that there is a bigger purpose at work in me, I am filled with unexplainable peace and joy.

Knowing that I am saved through grace and

belief in God's own son brings a great deal of relief and gratitude. My Lord, Jesus, is the reason I even have access to the Father at all. It's by Christ's work on the cross and the certainty that God raised him from the dead (Romans 10:9-10) that I know I am not only an image-bearer of God, but also a child of God.

DARING TO DREAM

"Every great dream begins with a dreamer. Always remember, you have within you the strength, the patience, and the passion to reach for the stars to change the world."

HARRIET TUBMAN

During those first precarious days in the hospital, as I got to know my nurses, physicians, orderlies, and various technicians, I was impressed by how much they cared, how hard they worked, and how much we all had in common. Behind the lab coats, masks, and stethoscopes, they were people just like you and me. And so many of them looked like they could just really use a break.

Shortly after my diagnosis, I had a vision of some sort of hospital ministry. I pictured a respite room dedicated to hospital workers, where they could meet with therapists or clergy, have a bite to eat, play a board game, practice mindfulness, or listen to music.

I even thought about sending a survey to local hospitals asking what healthcare staff would want to see in such a room. Unfortunately, I realized that I had neither the connections nor the resources to take that dream any further. So I decided to focus on another dream.

My other dream was to, at least in some small way, make another person's journey more bearable. All throughout my life, I have chosen to see trials and trauma through a unique lens, as an opportunity to comfort others with the comfort I myself have received from God (II Corinthians 1:4). In each case, I eventually came around to asking myself, "How can I use this to help someone else?" This most recent season of my life is no different.

Over the course of several months, I was often reminded of the phrase, "start small". This little book began as an expansion on a blog post I wrote in December 2022 entitled *Dealing with Difficulties.* I was encouraged in a number of different ways to keep writing, and so I did. I would wait, listen during my prayer time, and write. Wait, listen, write. That's how it went until I settled on what you have in your hands.

Many writers far more famous than I have written during terrible circumstances. The apostle Paul wrote much of the New Testament while imprisoned. Dr. Martin Luther King, Jr. wrote his famous *Letter from a Birmingham Jail* while unjustly detained. Dr. Viktor Frankl wrote ideas for his first book, *Man's Search for Meaning*, on little scraps of paper during his time in Nazi concentration camps. And John Piper wrote *Lessons From a Hospital Bed,* well, from a hospital bed.

All that to say: Despite your arduous circumstances, what you have to offer is important! Even if it's just in some small fashion, find a way to embrace hope. Find a way to capture courage. Don't give up on your dreams.

A FINAL WORD

"Have I not commanded you? Be strong and courageous. Do not be afraid; do not be discouraged, for the Lord your God will be with you wherever you go."

JOSHUA 1:9

Life has different seasons. Sometimes we simply need to pause and pivot. Other times, we need to listen to our bodies. Healthy self-care includes eating well, getting enough sleep, and having routine medical check-ups which may prove life-saving. Choosing a positive mindset, engaging in laughter, and seeking social support are all powerful ways to combat negative health outcomes.

Taking the time to find one's tribe of safe people, allowing others to help when needed, treating ourselves with compassion, and making space for spiritual integration can all be useful in distressing times. There are lessons to learn and dreams to pursue along the way. I hope you have found this small book to be of some encouragement during your journey.

REFERENCES

Bennett, E. (2020). *The Helper: Growing as an Enneagram 2*. Whitaker House.

Braman, L. (2020). Emotion Sensation Feeling Wheel. https://lindsaybraman.com/emotion-sensation-feeling-wheel/

Browning, E. B. (1850). *The Poems of Elizabeth Barrett Browning: With Memoir, Etc*. Warne.

Boylan, J. M., Tompkins, J. L., & Krueger, P. M. (2022). Psychological well-being, education, and mortality. *Health Psychology*, *41*(3), 225.

Cloud, H., & Townsend, J. (1996). *Safe people: How to find relationships that are good for you and avoid those that aren't*. Zondervan.

Crum, A. J., & Langer, E. J. (2007). Mind-set matters exercise and the placebo effect. *Psychological Science*, *18*(2), 165-171.

Crum, A. J., Salovey, P., & Achor, S. (2013).

Rethinking stress: the role of mindsets in determining the stress response. *Journal of personality and social psychology*, *104*(4), c716.

Gaines, J. (2023, Spring) Worth the Weight. *The Magnolia Journal Magazine*. *26*, p. 57.

Gračanin, A., Bylsma, L. M., & Vingerhoets, A. J. (2014). Is crying a self-soothing behavior?. *Frontiers in psychology*, *5*, 502.

Hopper, S. I., Murray, S. L., Ferrara, L. R., & Singleton, J. K. (2019). Effectiveness of diaphragmatic breathing for reducing physiological and psychological stress in adults: a quantitative systematic review. *JBI Evidence Synthesis*, *17*(9), 1855-1876.

Ingram, C. (n.d.). *The A.R.T. of Survival*. YouVersion | The
Bible App | Bible.com. https://www.bible.com/ reading-
plans/23393/day/2.

Jandu, B. (2020-2023), Various works. Pause & Ponder. https://barbarajandu.com/my-blog

Kabat-Zinn, J., & Hanh, T. N. (2009). *Full Catastrophe Living: Using the wisdom of your body and mind to face stress, pain, and illness*. Delta.

Lasseter, J. (2006). Cars [Motion Picture]. Walt Disney Pictures.

Lee, L. O., James, P., Zevon, E. S., Kim, E. S., Trudel-Fitzgerald, C., Spiro III, A., ... & Kubzansky, L. D. (2019). Optimism is associated with exceptional longevity in 2 epidemiologic cohorts of men and women. *Proceedings of the National Academy of Sciences, 116*(37), 18357-18362.

Lewis, C. S. (1959). *Mere Christianity* (2nd ed., p. 114). MacMillan.

Lindahl, E., Tilton, K., Eickholt, N., & Ferguson-Stegall, L. (2016). Yoga reduces perceived stress and exhaustion levels in healthy elderly individuals. *Complementary Therapies in Clinical Practice, 24*, 50-56.

Manske, J. & Manske, J. (2005). Needs Wheel. Nonviolent Communication for the Next Generation. https://nvcnextgen.org/nvc-handouts/

Nagoski, E., & Amelia Nagoski, D. M. A. (2020). *Burnout: The secret to unlocking the stress cycle*. Ballantine Books.

Obama, M. (2022). *The Light We Carry: Overcoming in Uncertain Times*. Crown.

Pasricha, P.J. (2023) The Brain-Gut Connection. Johns Hopkins Medicine. https://

www.hopkinsmedicine.org/health/wellness-and-prevention/the-brain-gut-connection

Pressman, S. D., Acevedo, A. M., Hammond, K. V., & Kraft-Feil, T. L. (2021). Smile (or grimace) through the pain? The effects of experimentally manipulated facial expressions on needle-injection responses. *Emotion (Washington, D.C.)*, *21*(6), 1188–1203.

Rosenbloom, M. H., Schmahmann, J. D., & Price, B. H. (2012). The functional neuroanatomy of decision-making. *The Journal of neuropsychiatry and clinical neurosciences*, *24*(3), 266-277.

Savage, B. M., Lujan, H. L., Thipparthi, R. R., & DiCarlo, S. E. (2017). Humor, laughter, learning, and health! A brief review. *Advances in physiology education*.

Shapiro, S. L. (2020). Good Morning, I Love You: Mindfulness and Self-compassion Practices to Rewire Your Brain for Calm, Clarity, and Joy.

Taylor, S. E. (2011). Social support: A review. *The Oxford handbook of health psychology*, *1*, **189-214.**

Townsend, J. (2015). *The Entitlement Cure: Finding Success at Work and in Relationships in a Shortcut World*. Zondervan.

Uvnäs-Moberg, K., Handlin, L., & Petersson, M. (2015). Self-soothing behaviors with particular reference to oxytocin release induced by non-noxious sensory stimulation. *Frontiers in psychology*, *5*, 1529.

West, J., Otte, C., Geher, K., Johnson, J., & Mohr, D. C. (2004). Effects of Hatha yoga and African dance on perceived stress, affect, and salivary cortisol. *Annals of Behavioral Medicine*, *28*(2), 114-118.

ACKNOWLEDGEMENTS

I truly appreciate you, my dear husband and sons, for your constant love, support, hugs, and laughter. I love you all so much, and couldn't imagine doing life without my sweet 'fam-bam'.

A special thanks to you, my "brutal but brilliant" editor, Orion. Without you, this book could not be published. May God bless you in your future career as a writer.

Thank you, Renée (artbyreneeswitkes.com), for the beautiful cover art: Cyclamen Persicum; Empathetic Devoted Heart. May God's grace cover you in all areas of your life.

Thank you Tina and Megan for encouraging me to write this book, and thank you Susana, and Joy for supporting me in so many ways throughout my process.

And my deepest gratitude to everyone in my tribe who continue to check in on me, encourage me, have tea with me, and pray for me. You are my people.

ABOUT THE AUTHOR

Barbara Jandu

Barbara earned her master's degree at Santa Clara University in Counseling Psychology with an emphasis in Health Psychology. She works as a therapist and writes a monthly blog called Pause and Ponder. Prior to becoming a therapist, her professional experience included management, staffing, and children's ministry. Barbara enjoys reading historical fiction, traveling, and cooking. She and her husband have been married for over 20 years and live in California with their two sons.

45649768R00069